TANGLED SHAKESPEARE

A Midsummer Night's Dream

By
MKAY B B WATSON

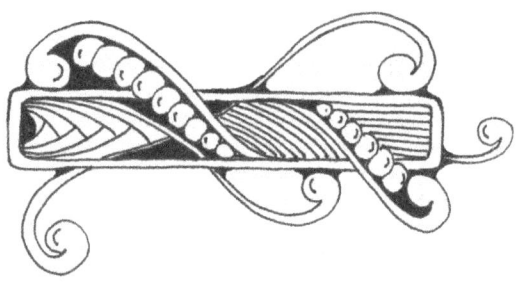

Copyright © 2019 by Mary Kay Watson

All rights reserved. No part of this publication may be reproduced, distributed or transmitted in any form or by any means, including photocopying, recording or other electronic or mechanical methods, without the prior written permission of the publisher, except in the case of brief quotations embodied in reviews and certain other non-commercial uses permitted by copyright law.

For permission requests please contact
Canoe Tree Press.

Published 2019

Printed in the United States of America
Print ISBN: 978-0-578-47679-7

Publisher Information:
Canoe Tree Press
PO Box 867
Manchester, VT 05254

www.CanoeTreePress.com

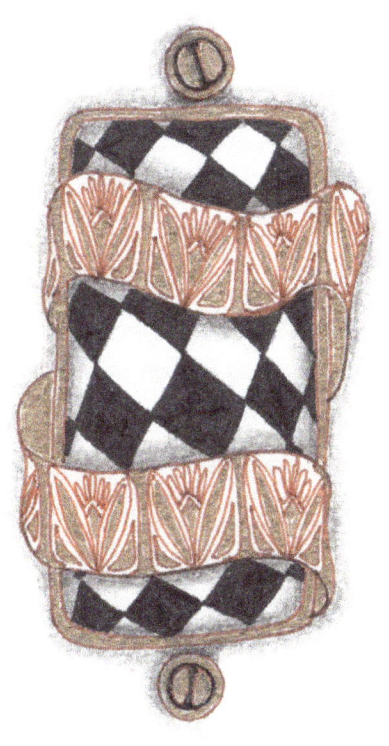

To my Muse, Dennis,
and my Maeves, Meg and Amy

Oberon, King of the Faeries

"The course of true love never did run smooth".

> Act I Scene I
> Lysander to Hermia

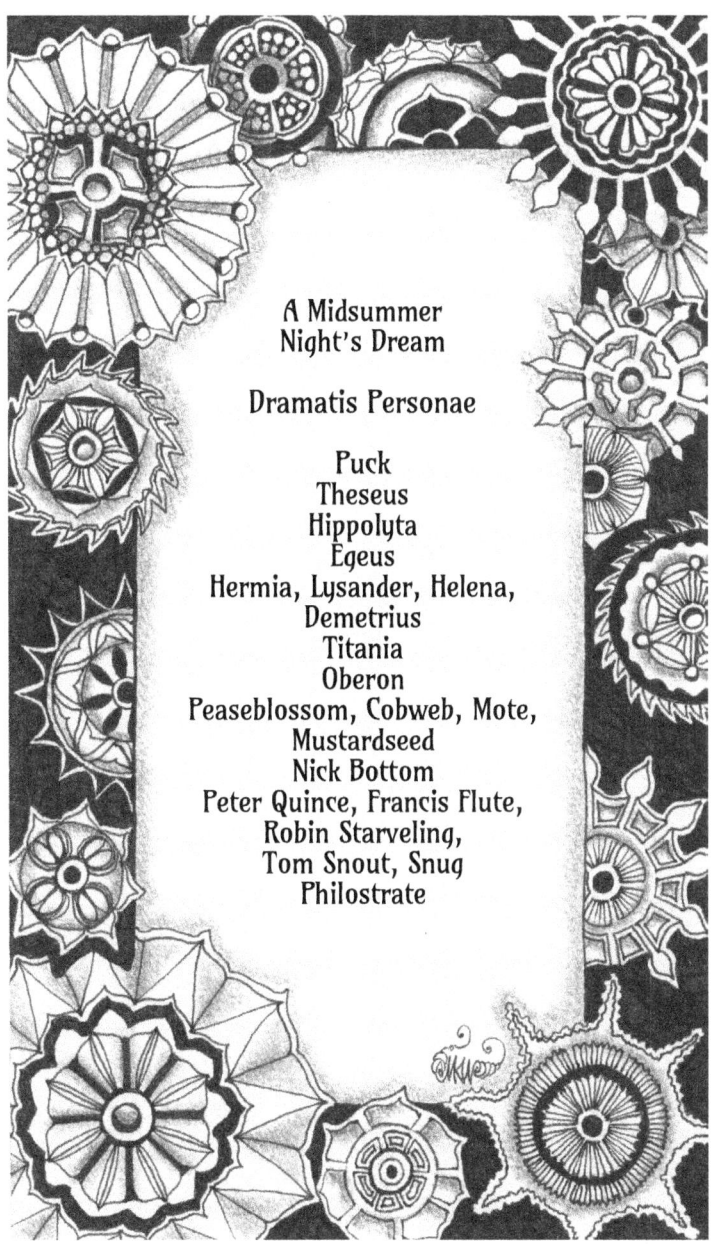

A Midsummer
Night's Dream

Dramatis Personae

Puck
Theseus
Hippolyta
Egeus
Hermia, Lysander, Helena,
Demetrius
Titania
Oberon
Peaseblossom, Cobweb, Mote,
Mustardseed
Nick Bottom
Peter Quince, Francis Flute,
Robin Starveling,
Tom Snout, Snug
Philostrate

Theseus, Duke of Athens and his bride, the captured, Amazonian Queen, Hippolyta.

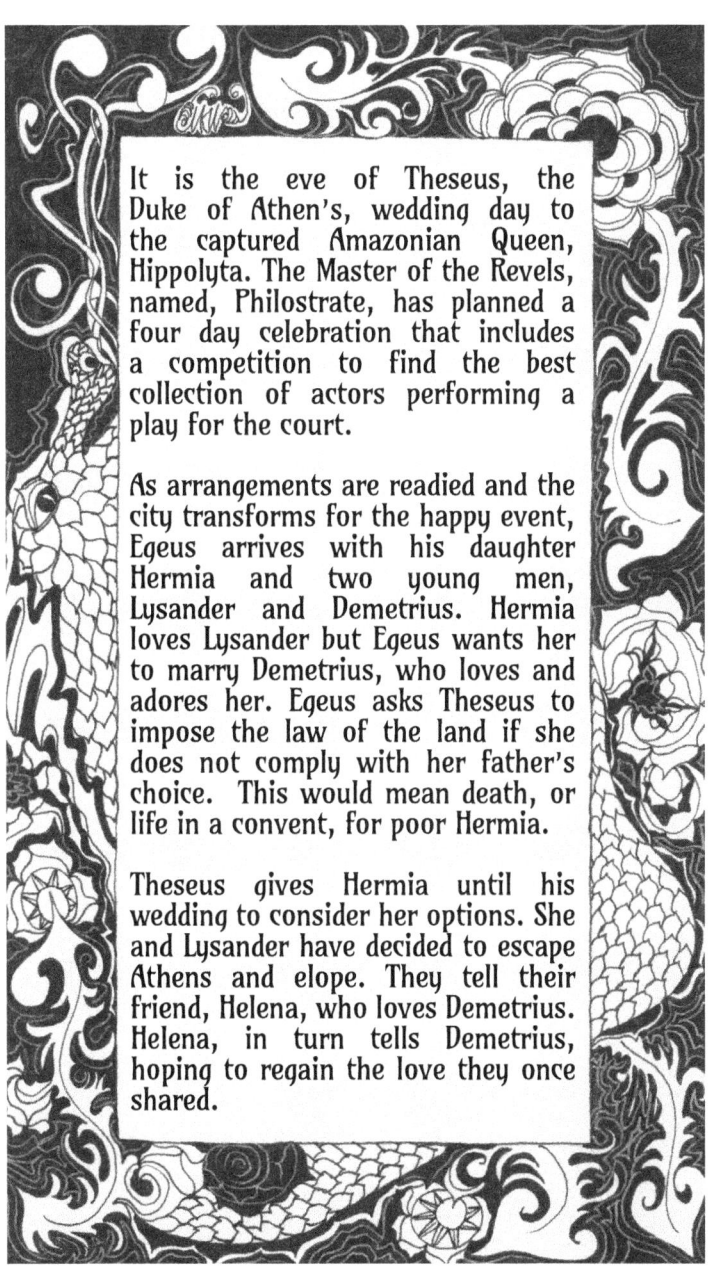

It is the eve of Theseus, the Duke of Athen's, wedding day to the captured Amazonian Queen, Hippolyta. The Master of the Revels, named, Philostrate, has planned a four day celebration that includes a competition to find the best collection of actors performing a play for the court.

As arrangements are readied and the city transforms for the happy event, Egeus arrives with his daughter Hermia and two young men, Lysander and Demetrius. Hermia loves Lysander but Egeus wants her to marry Demetrius, who loves and adores her. Egeus asks Theseus to impose the law of the land if she does not comply with her father's choice. This would mean death, or life in a convent, for poor Hermia.

Theseus gives Hermia until his wedding to consider her options. She and Lysander have decided to escape Athens and elope. They tell their friend, Helena, who loves Demetrius. Helena, in turn tells Demetrius, hoping to regain the love they once shared.

Egeus, Hermia's father

Egeus, brings Hermia to Theseus, for his judgement on her choice of suitors

Lysander, Hermia's true love

Demetrius. Egeus wants his daughter, Hermia, to marry Demetrius.

Helena, friend to Hermia and Lysander. She loves Demetrius.

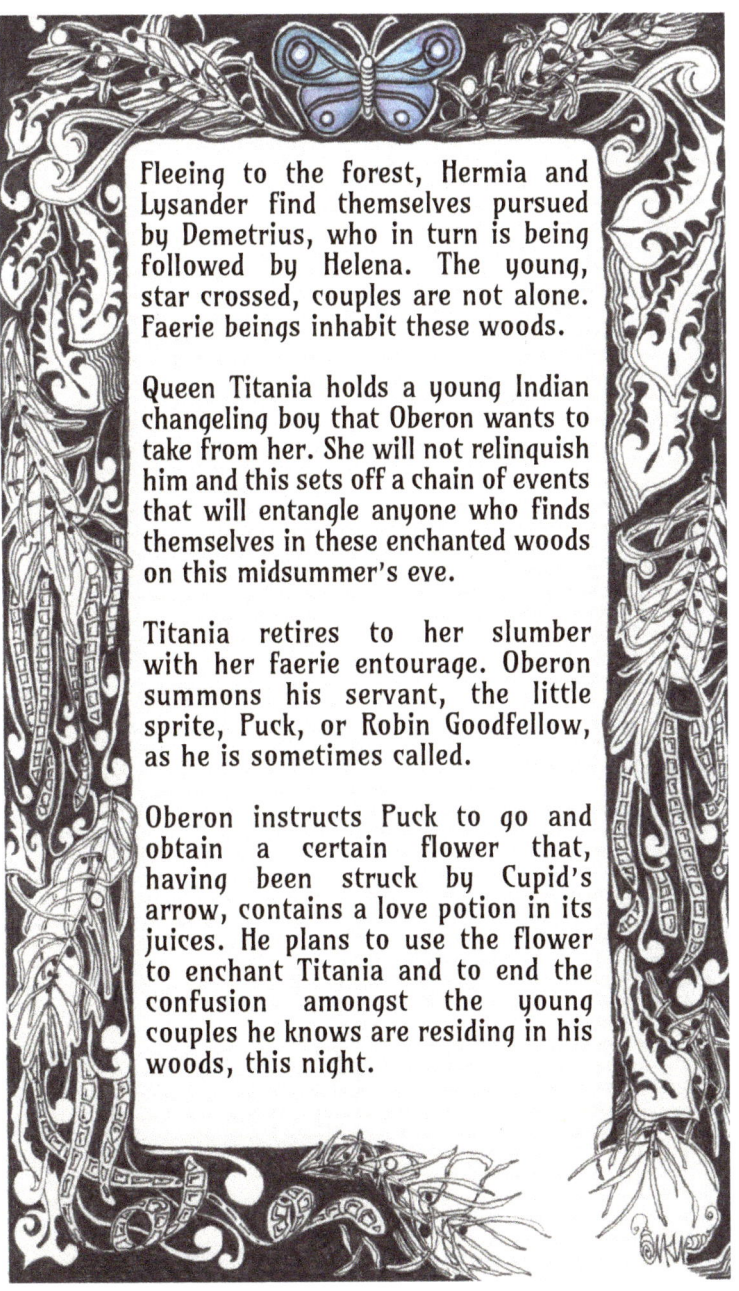

Fleeing to the forest, Hermia and Lysander find themselves pursued by Demetrius, who in turn is being followed by Helena. The young, star crossed, couples are not alone. Faerie beings inhabit these woods.

Queen Titania holds a young Indian changeling boy that Oberon wants to take from her. She will not relinquish him and this sets off a chain of events that will entangle anyone who finds themselves in these enchanted woods on this midsummer's eve.

Titania retires to her slumber with her faerie entourage. Oberon summons his servant, the little sprite, Puck, or Robin Goodfellow, as he is sometimes called.

Oberon instructs Puck to go and obtain a certain flower that, having been struck by Cupid's arrow, contains a love potion in its juices. He plans to use the flower to enchant Titania and to end the confusion amongst the young couples he knows are residing in his woods, this night.

Titania,
Queen of the Faeries

Puck, also goes by the name
Robin Goodfellow.

I know a bank where the
wild thyme blows,
Where oxlips and the
nodding violet grows,
Quite over-canopied with
luscious woodbine,
With sweet musk-roses and
with eglantine.

Oberon instructs Puck where
he will find Queen Titania
and her faerie entourage.

Cobweb

Mustardseed

Mote, often called Moth

Peaseblossom

Unnamed faerie

Unnamed faerie

Unnamed faerie

Unnamed faerie

Unnamed faerie

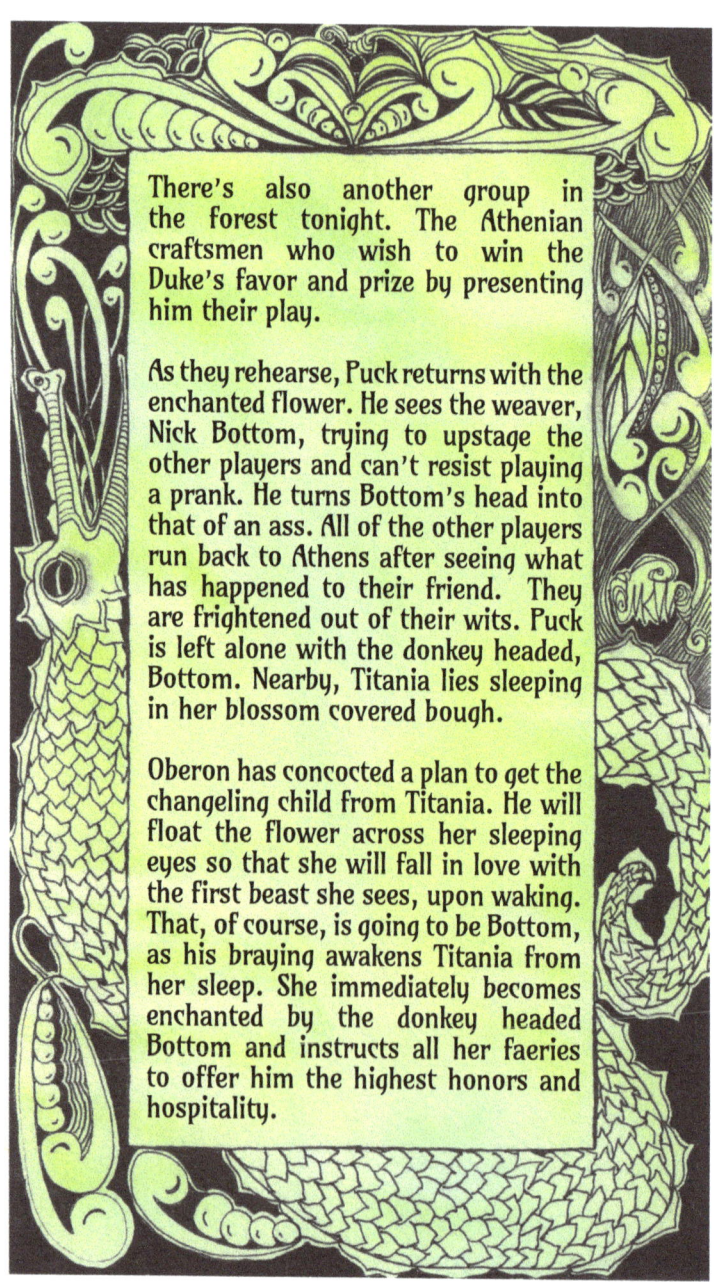

There's also another group in the forest tonight. The Athenian craftsmen who wish to win the Duke's favor and prize by presenting him their play.

As they rehearse, Puck returns with the enchanted flower. He sees the weaver, Nick Bottom, trying to upstage the other players and can't resist playing a prank. He turns Bottom's head into that of an ass. All of the other players run back to Athens after seeing what has happened to their friend. They are frightened out of their wits. Puck is left alone with the donkey headed, Bottom. Nearby, Titania lies sleeping in her blossom covered bough.

Oberon has concocted a plan to get the changeling child from Titania. He will float the flower across her sleeping eyes so that she will fall in love with the first beast she sees, upon waking. That, of course, is going to be Bottom, as his braying awakens Titania from her sleep. She immediately becomes enchanted by the donkey headed Bottom and instructs all her faeries to offer him the highest honors and hospitality.

Nick Bottom, after Puck changes his head into that of a donkey's.

Under Oberon's enchanted flower spell, Titania awakens from her slumber and immediately falls in love with the donkey headed Bottom.

Nick Bottom evokes
confidence as an ass.

Puck finds Hermia and Lysander asleep in the forest and uses the love potion on Lysander by mistake.

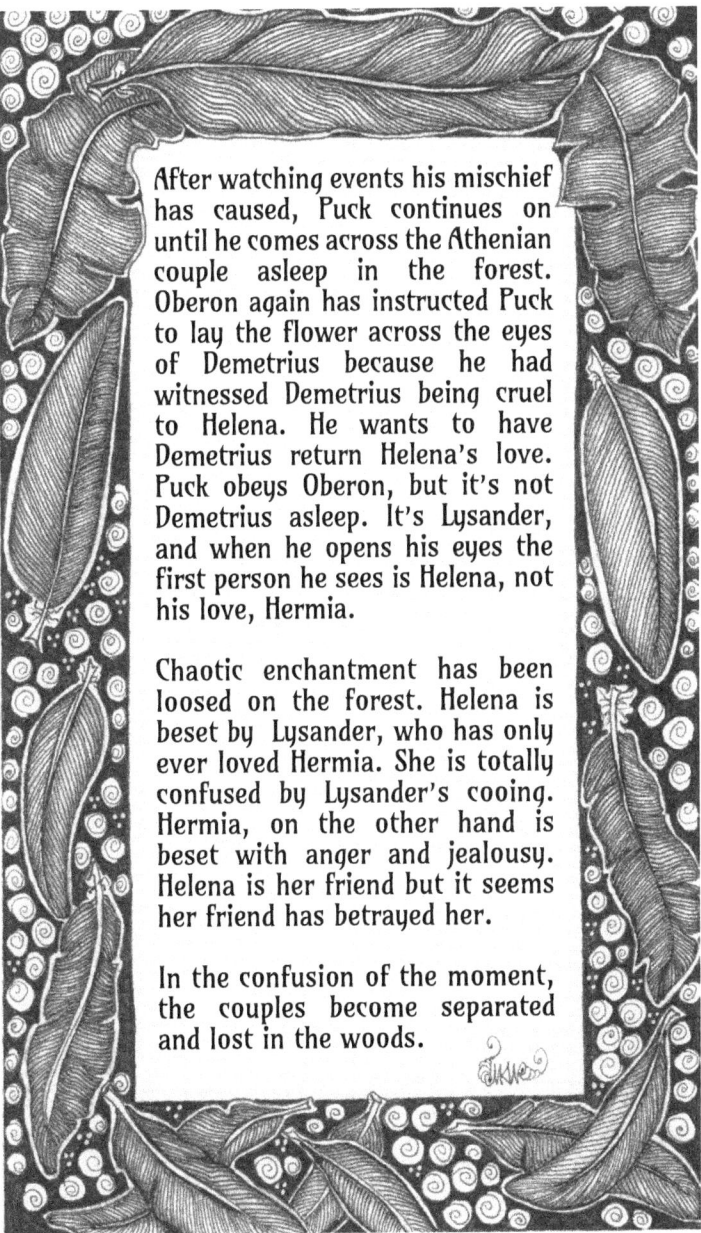

After watching events his mischief has caused, Puck continues on until he comes across the Athenian couple asleep in the forest. Oberon again has instructed Puck to lay the flower across the eyes of Demetrius because he had witnessed Demetrius being cruel to Helena. He wants to have Demetrius return Helena's love. Puck obeys Oberon, but it's not Demetrius asleep. It's Lysander, and when he opens his eyes the first person he sees is Helena, not his love, Hermia.

Chaotic enchantment has been loosed on the forest. Helena is beset by Lysander, who has only ever loved Hermia. She is totally confused by Lysander's cooing. Hermia, on the other hand is beset with anger and jealousy. Helena is her friend but it seems her friend has betrayed her.

In the confusion of the moment, the couples become separated and lost in the woods.

Helena begs Demetrius for his love.

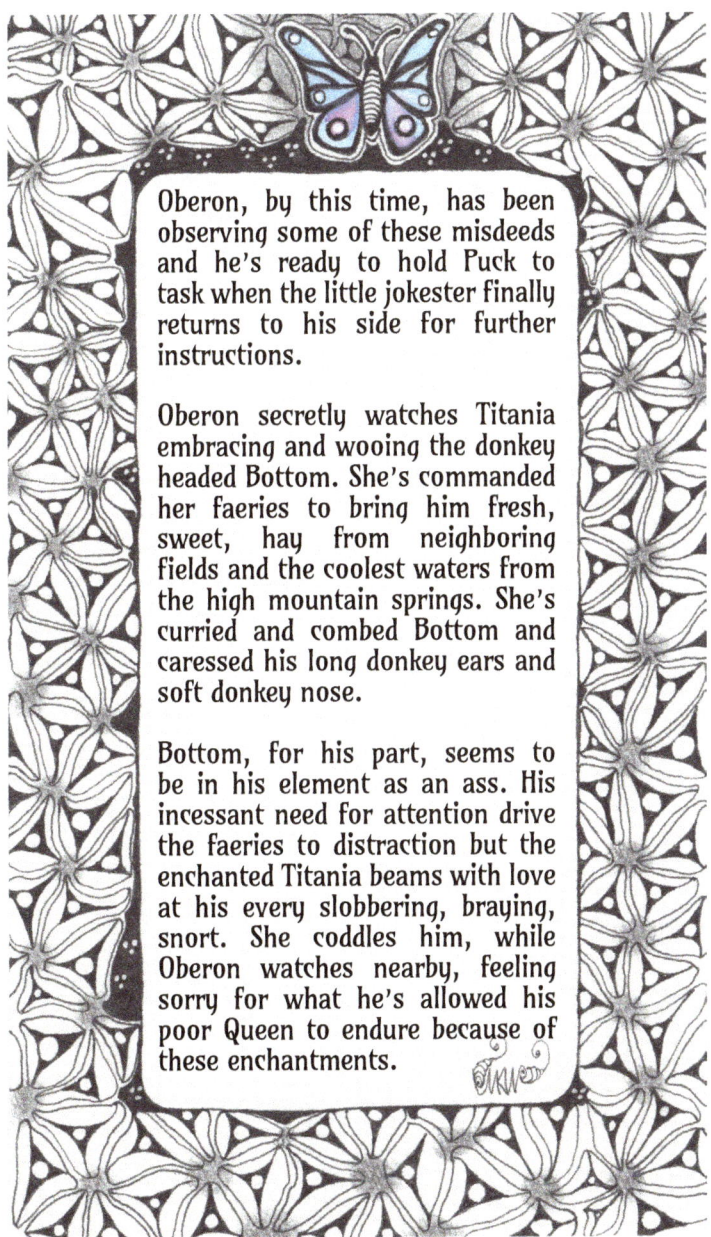

Oberon, by this time, has been observing some of these misdeeds and he's ready to hold Puck to task when the little jokester finally returns to his side for further instructions.

Oberon secretly watches Titania embracing and wooing the donkey headed Bottom. She's commanded her faeries to bring him fresh, sweet, hay from neighboring fields and the coolest waters from the high mountain springs. She's curried and combed Bottom and caressed his long donkey ears and soft donkey nose.

Bottom, for his part, seems to be in his element as an ass. His incessant need for attention drive the faeries to distraction but the enchanted Titania beams with love at his every slobbering, braying, snort. She coddles him, while Oberon watches nearby, feeling sorry for what he's allowed his poor Queen to endure because of these enchantments.

Titania nuzzling Bottom. The magic flower, love potion has blinded her to the fact that he is literally and figuratively...an ass.

Puck rejoins Oberon and they watch together all of the antics going on in this forest.

Oberon instructs Puck how to remedy the mess Puck made with the love potion and the Athenian couples.

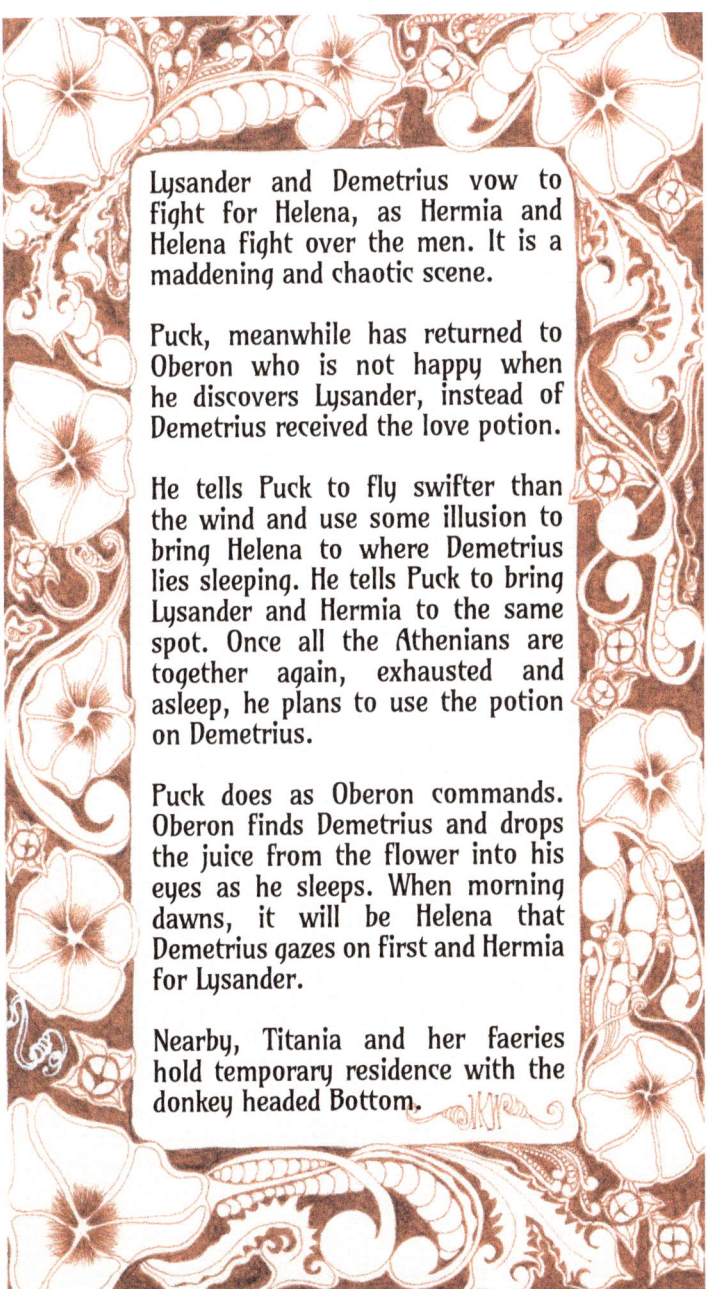

Lysander and Demetrius vow to fight for Helena, as Hermia and Helena fight over the men. It is a maddening and chaotic scene.

Puck, meanwhile has returned to Oberon who is not happy when he discovers Lysander, instead of Demetrius received the love potion.

He tells Puck to fly swifter than the wind and use some illusion to bring Helena to where Demetrius lies sleeping. He tells Puck to bring Lysander and Hermia to the same spot. Once all the Athenians are together again, exhausted and asleep, he plans to use the potion on Demetrius.

Puck does as Oberon commands. Oberon finds Demetrius and drops the juice from the flower into his eyes as he sleeps. When morning dawns, it will be Helena that Demetrius gazes on first and Hermia for Lysander.

Nearby, Titania and her faeries hold temporary residence with the donkey headed Bottom.

A fight ensues between Hermia and Helena. The result of so much chaos and confusion over who loves whom.

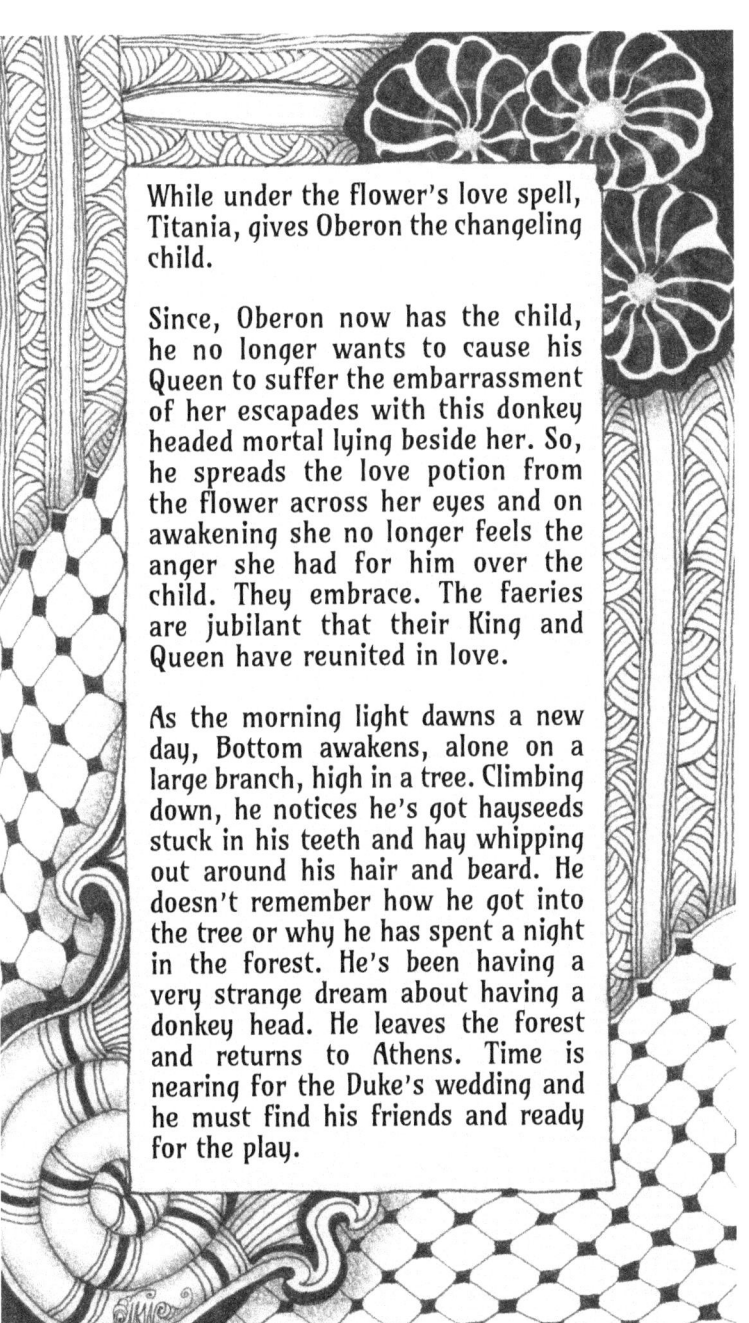

While under the flower's love spell, Titania, gives Oberon the changeling child.

Since, Oberon now has the child, he no longer wants to cause his Queen to suffer the embarrassment of her escapades with this donkey headed mortal lying beside her. So, he spreads the love potion from the flower across her eyes and on awakening she no longer feels the anger she had for him over the child. They embrace. The faeries are jubilant that their King and Queen have reunited in love.

As the morning light dawns a new day, Bottom awakens, alone on a large branch, high in a tree. Climbing down, he notices he's got hayseeds stuck in his teeth and hay whipping out around his hair and beard. He doesn't remember how he got into the tree or why he has spent a night in the forest. He's been having a very strange dream about having a donkey head. He leaves the forest and returns to Athens. Time is nearing for the Duke's wedding and he must find his friends and ready for the play.

The couples finally end up in the same area of forest and fall asleep from exhaustion. They are unaware that Puck and Oberon have orchestrated the evening events.

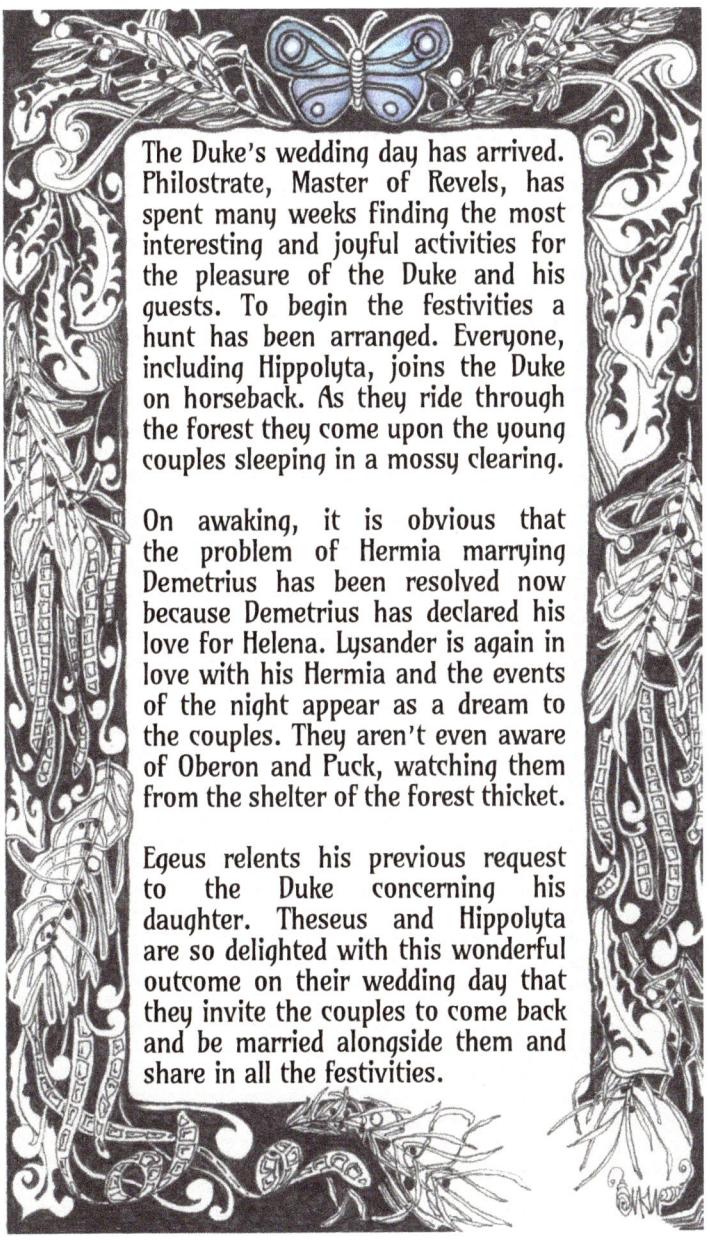

The Duke's wedding day has arrived. Philostrate, Master of Revels, has spent many weeks finding the most interesting and joyful activities for the pleasure of the Duke and his guests. To begin the festivities a hunt has been arranged. Everyone, including Hippolyta, joins the Duke on horseback. As they ride through the forest they come upon the young couples sleeping in a mossy clearing.

On awaking, it is obvious that the problem of Hermia marrying Demetrius has been resolved now because Demetrius has declared his love for Helena. Lysander is again in love with his Hermia and the events of the night appear as a dream to the couples. They aren't even aware of Oberon and Puck, watching them from the shelter of the forest thicket.

Egeus relents his previous request to the Duke concerning his daughter. Theseus and Hippolyta are so delighted with this wonderful outcome on their wedding day that they invite the couples to come back and be married alongside them and share in all the festivities.

Titania has come to Athens to bestow her blessings on Theseus and Hippolyta on their wedding day.

Queen Hippolyta and
Theseus, Duke of Athens on
their wedding day.

Demetrius and Helena,
wedded.

Hermia and Lysander, wedded

Tom Snout, the tinker, in his costume to play "Wall".

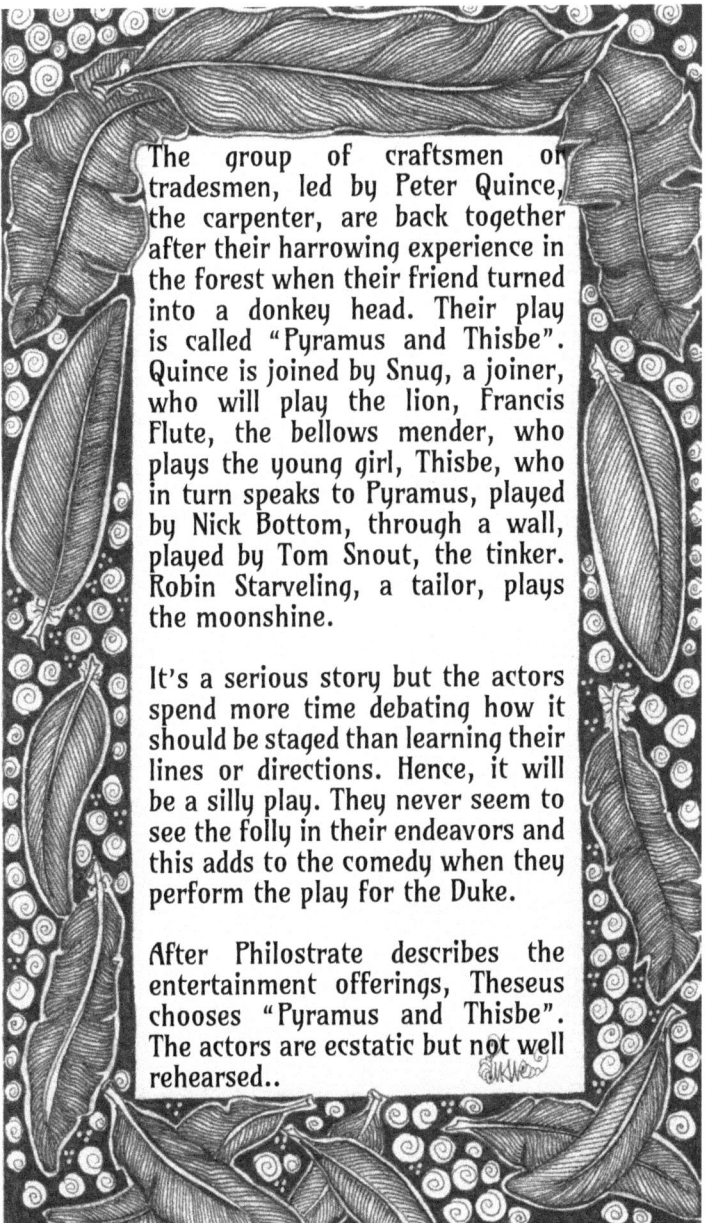

The group of craftsmen or tradesmen, led by Peter Quince, the carpenter, are back together after their harrowing experience in the forest when their friend turned into a donkey head. Their play is called "Pyramus and Thisbe". Quince is joined by Snug, a joiner, who will play the lion, Francis Flute, the bellows mender, who plays the young girl, Thisbe, who in turn speaks to Pyramus, played by Nick Bottom, through a wall, played by Tom Snout, the tinker. Robin Starveling, a tailor, plays the moonshine.

It's a serious story but the actors spend more time debating how it should be staged than learning their lines or directions. Hence, it will be a silly play. They never seem to see the folly in their endeavors and this adds to the comedy when they perform the play for the Duke.

After Philostrate describes the entertainment offerings, Theseus chooses "Pyramus and Thisbe". The actors are ecstatic but not well rehearsed..

Nick Bottom dressed as
"Pyramus".

Snug, the joiner, as "Lion".

Robin Starveling, the tailor, as "Moonshine."

Francis Flute, the bellows mender, reluctantly, playing the young lady "Thisbe."

Peter Quince, leader and organizer of the actors in this group of craftsmen.

Philostrate, Master of the Revels, responsible for all of the wedding festivities and entertainment.

King Oberon and Queen Titania, with their faerie entourage, join the mortals at the ending of the day's festivities. Unseen, they watch as the play, "Pyramus and Thisbe", comes to its conclusion and the mortals remove themselves to their bedchambers.

The faerie procession then follows the young couples to their doors and blesses their unions. Puck, then turns to you, the audience, dear reader, and speaks directly.

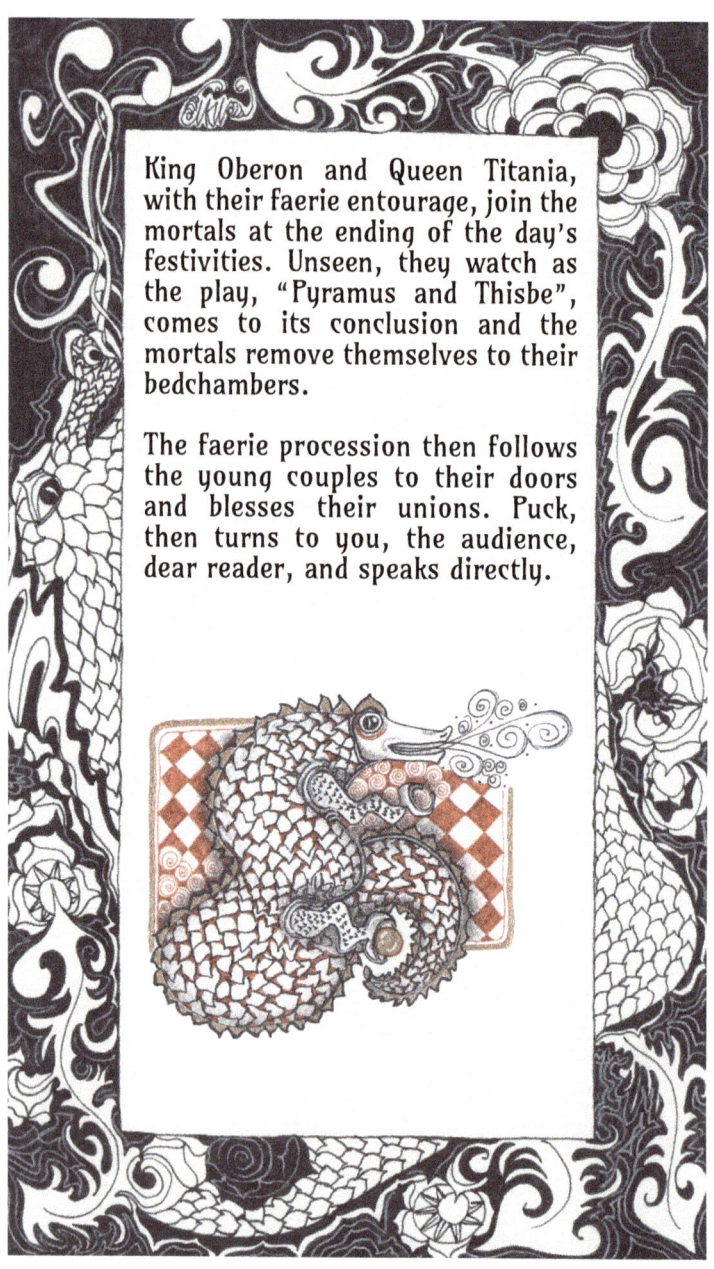

Oberon and Titania take their seats to secretly watch the wedding festivities along side the mortals.

Faerie processional.

If we shadows have offended,
Think but this, and all is mended,
That you have but slumber'd here
While these visions did appear.
And this weak and idle theme,
No more yielding but a dream,
Gentles, do not reprehend:
if you pardon, we will mend:
And, as I am an honest Puck,
If we have unearned luck
Now to 'scape the serpent's tongue,
We will make amends ere long;
Else the Puck a liar call;
So, good night unto you all.
Give me your hands, if we be friends,
And Robin shall restore amends.

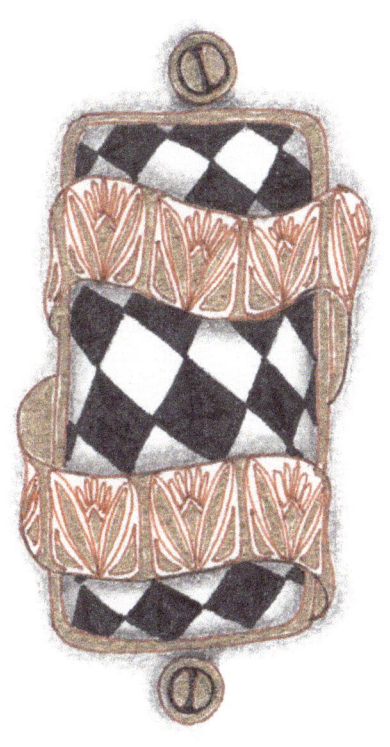

"Lord, what fools these mortals be"!
Act III Scene II
Puck to Oberon

With a lifetime of drawing behind me, I decided it was time to combine my passion for drawing with my love of Shakespeare. "Tangled Shakespeare" is the result. I want to introduce Shakespeare in a way that's easy to understand, but gloriously done in brightly colored designs. Like the productions of the plays I've seen, I want my characters to express the nature of a play. To bring the words to life and give them emotion. I want my audience to get lost in the details of the drawings, a feast for the senses, just like a staged production. Most of all, I want my audience to enjoy Shakespeare.

An accomplished drafts person and watercolorist, I also teach the Zentangle® Method of drawing, created by Rick Roberts and Maria Thomas. As a Certified Zentangle Teacher I am able to teach students who have no drawing experience, beautiful patterns, like the ones in this book. Find more information at zentangle.com

Follow MKay B B Watson and her Shakespeare characters on tangledshakespeare.com.

www.ingramcontent.com/pod-product-compliance
Lightning Source LLC
Chambersburg PA
CBHW062028290426
44108CB00025B/2822